Original title:
Existentialism for Dummies

Copyright © 2025 Creative Arts Management OÜ
All rights reserved.

Author: Matthew Whitaker
ISBN HARDBACK: 978-1-80566-029-3
ISBN PAPERBACK: 978-1-80566-324-9

Chasing Fleeting Moments

A squirrel darts, I miss the thrill,
Life zips by, oh what a pill.
I blink and poof, it's all a blur,
Was that a thought? Or just a slur?

My coffee's cold, my mind's on fire,
Chasing dreams that won't acquire.
Ticking clocks make me a mess,
What does it mean? I couldn't guess.

Chronicles of the Wandering Mind

I ponder deep while washing socks,
Is there meaning in my blocks?
Each lost thought's an expedition,
To nowhere, fun—my weird condition.

My cat stares hard in silent glee,
What secrets hide beyond the tree?
She knows it all, or so I think,
I fetch a snack, then start to sink.

The Silence Between the Notes

I hum a tune that feels like air,
Yet somehow ends up everywhere.
In pauses loud, my head's a mess,
Do notes need rest? Or just caress?

The music stops, what now? I sigh,
Is silence just a tricky lie?
The gaps between can dance and sway,
Or turn my thoughts to shades of gray.

Whispers of the Unseen

I question clouds, do they feel free?
Are shadows sad? Let's wait and see.
Invisible thoughts tap on my door,
Saying, 'Hey, you're smart, but why encore?'

I laugh at life, it chuckles back,
In silly hats, we share a snack.
Unseen whispers float in the breeze,
Explaining why I worry with ease.

Philosophers in Pajamas

In their cozy PJs, they ponder deep,
Wondering why the fish just won't leap.
Socrates spills coffee, makes a big mess,
While Descartes debates, in his old dress.

Aristotle's snoring disrupts the night,
While Kant starts to argue about what's right.
With blankets sagging and thoughts so grand,
These thinkers are lost, yet still understand.

A Tapestry of Ephemeral Dreams

Dreams weave around like a colorful kite,
Slipping through fingers, what a funny sight!
A philosopher laughs as he counts the sheep,
Claiming they have secrets, hidden so deep.

Hedonists party on thin strands of air,
While realists wonder if they're really there.
A tapestry woven of laughter and sighs,
In the land of dreams, the absurd always flies.

Musings on Mortality

Why fret, my friend, about the final bow?
Life's just a joke, take a silly vow.
Tick-tock goes the clock, why worry at all?
One day we're here, then we trip and fall.

The worm now laughs, wearing glasses so thick,
Reading the book of life, what a funny trick!
So raise a toast to the stars up high,
For we're just brief flickers in the cosmic pie.

Nonsense in the Cosmos

Galaxies dance in a whimsical trance,
Planets wear hats and invite you to dance.
Stars play poker with light-years to spare,
While asteroids giggle at a comet's wild hair.

Black holes are moody, they swallow the light,
Outer space parties last all through the night.
With a wink and a nod, the universe hums,
In the realm of nonsense, delight always comes.

Roads Less Traveled

Two paths diverge in a snack-filled maze,
One leads to wisdom, the other to haze.
Pick a route adorned with laughter galore,
Or find yourself pondering what you're here for.

Whichever you choose, don't fret in strife,
Turn every wrong turn into a new life.
For life's a wild ride on a fumble-filled road,
And out of the chaos, true joy can erode.

A Dreamer's Confession

Last night I dreamt I was made of cheese,
Woke up confused, feeling pretty uneased.
Am I just a snack or an ungraspable thought?
A buffet of questions that I never sought.

Between bites of camembert and a slice of brie,
I pondered my purpose, while nibbling with glee.
Life's just a platter where nothing is real,
So grab a fork, my friend, and see how you feel.

Conversations with the Cosmos

I looked to the stars for signs of my fate,
They twinkled and giggled, 'You're never too late!'
"Are we just atoms?" I asked in despair,
They winked back at me, "Who really would care?"

With each floating thought I felt light as a breeze,
The universe chuckled, "Relax and just squeeze."
A cosmic charade where no answers exist,
Let's dance with the void, and laugh at the mist.

Absurdity in Everyday Life

Woke up this morning, socks didn't match,
Coffee spilled over, like a comedic catch.
I tripped on a cat while my plans went astray,
Welcome to life – it's a bizarre cabaret!

Searching for meaning in a sock drawer calamity,
Finding deep truths in mundane insanity.
So, let's toast to the quirks in our chaotic strife,
For in the absurd, we just might find life.

The Weight of Questions

Why are we here, oh what a shock,
Do ducks ponder fate on their daily walk?
Is pizza life's answer, or just a slice?
Sometimes I wonder, then think it's nice.

The universe laughs, a cosmic joke,
While we fumble with truths, like a puzzled bloke.
I ask my cat, but she just purrs,
So I guess I'll stick to my daily burrs.

Shadows of Purpose

Why bother with plans, when we can just glide,
Like jellybeans rolling in a tricky tide?
Do we dance for a reason or just for the fun?
Maybe life's just a game, silly but done.

In shadows we fumble, like kids on a spree,
With questions flailing, 'what's the key?'
But maybe the key is just being awed,
By nothing at all, how utterly flawed.

A Beginner's Guide to Being

Wake up each morning, hoping to find,
A map to the meaning, but it's just blind.
Do I dig in the garden, or take a long nap?
These thoughts weigh me down like a sleepy trap.

Let's splash in the puddles, push thoughts out of sight,
Who needs deep meaning when it's sunny and bright?
Grab a cupcake, a cookie, or two,
Being is tricky, but tastes good, who knew?

What Makes Us Whole

Does being whole mean less pizza to eat?
Or more midnight snacks, oh what a treat?
Do socks have feelings when they lose their mates?
I ponder the world and its quirky fates.

With laughter as glue, we stick in a mess,
Finding our wholeness in chaos, I guess.
For in every stumble and logical fall,
We giggle and grow, and perhaps that's it all.

A Symphony of Questions

Why do we exist, oh what a plight?
Can a toaster know love, or just toast all night?
If I talk to my goldfish, is he really there?
Or am I just nuts, with thoughts in the air?

What's the reason for socks, when they always stray?
Are the mismatched ones just trying to play?
If my chair could talk, would it spill all my beans?
Or keep all my secrets, as silent machines?

Do ants have a purpose, or just march in line?
Does my cat hold the secret to sipping fine wine?
If I laugh at my shadow, does it laugh too?
Or just roll its eyes, like shadows often do?

Is reality real, or just an old joke?
A sitcom we watch, and the world's just a smoke?
If we trip on a thought, do we land on a dream?
Or just wake up confused, lost in the scheme?

When Certainty Fades

Am I just a ghost, in a glitchy old game?
Or the hero who's lost, in a wild, wild fame?
Every glance at my watch, seems to whisper and chime,
What if time is just pizza, sliced up a rhyme?

When I open my door, is it me that I see?
Or a version of me, sipping coffee with glee?
If I squint at the stars, making shapes with my mind,
Do they come down for tea, or just leave me behind?

Are clouds just the thoughts of the sky on a spree?
Or does the sun play fetch, with the earth and the sea?
If my phone starts to think, will it text me in code?
Or just play me a tune, on its own little road?

When the fridge door is open, where does coolness go?
Is it just taking breaks, putting on a show?
In a world full of answers, I chuckle and grin,
For in questions we find that the fun can begin!

The Lightness of Being Lost

In a world with no map, I roam,
Chasing shadows, far from home.
Every dead end feels so right,
Stumbling through the day and night.

Directions? Please, I'll pass,
Life's a puzzle made of glass.
Falling into every pit,
A glorious, silly, cosmic fit.

Existence like a borrowed shoe,
Left foot wrong, but what's the view?
Laughter echoes, oh what fun,
In the race where all have run.

Is there a point, or just a jest?
I'll toast my fate with zest,
For being lost is quite the breeze,
While the universe laughs with ease.

When the Clock Stops

Tick-tock, what does it mean?
Time, a slippery, sneaky sheen.
When the clocks all stop and stare,
Do we breathe, or just declare?

Seconds pause, and I just grin,
What happens now? Just dive in.
Chasing minutes turns to dust,
In this stillness, laugh we must.

Pondering life's circus ride,
Do seconds knowledge ever provide?
Yet laughter's ring fills the air,
In whimsical wonders, we declare.

Clock hands frozen, what a show!
Let's dance in chaos, to and fro.
In this timeless, funny plight,
We find our joy in endless night.

Echoes of a Silent Mind

In the quiet where thoughts may stray,
Whispers dance, come out to play.
Silence speaks, but who's the host?
A party of one, yet I'm the ghost.

My mind's a theater, breaks the rules,
With empty seats for all the fools.
Ideas bounce like a rubber ball,
Crashing softly, do they recall?

I wear my crazy like a crown,
Thinking deeply, yet feeling down.
What's the point of all this fun?
Echoes giggle, "You are the one."

Quiet chaos wraps me tight,
In the rush, I find my flight.
From nothingness, pure joy I find,
In the echoes of my silent mind.

Dancing with Uncertainty

On a floor that creaks and sighs,
I twirl beneath uncertain skies.
With every step, I laugh and trip,
In wobbly shoes, I take a dip.

Life's a dance, all out of sync,
With every stomp, I rethink.
Is there rhythm, or a plan?
Just wobble wide, and take a stand.

Partners change with each new spin,
In this waltz, it's awkward gin.
But laughter whispers, "Don't be coy!"
Embrace the wobble, cherish the joy.

So here I sway in cosmic dance,
In misstep, I find my chance.
With uncertainty, my partner dear,
I laugh, I twirl, I have no fear.

Floating Through the Fog of Life

I drift on clouds made of cotton candy,
Each thought like a goldfish, slippery and dandy.
The world is a joke, and I'm just the punchline,
Trying to find meaning, but I've lost my timeline.

Embrace the chaos, it's all pretty wild,
With questions that dance like a giggling child.
I laugh at the chaos, the absurd and bizarre,
Hoping to find truth in a chocolate bar.

The Burden of Awareness

I woke up today, oh what a delight,
To ponder existence, under morning light.
Why are we here? Do we matter at all?
Ask the houseplant, it won't take my call.

I juggle my thoughts like a clown at a fair,
With balloons full of wonder, drifting in air.
The world's a stage, or maybe a sitcom,
Where the audience giggles, 'Hey, what's going on?'

Letters to an Invisible Friend

Dear imaginary buddy, are you still around?
I've penned you some letters, but they make no sound.
You never reply, but that's part of the game,
Life's a fun riddle, but without the fame.

I spill all my secrets, like beans from a can,
You nod with a smile, oh, you're such a fan.
We'll solve the universe or just share our snacks,
As we laugh at the chaos and dodge all the quacks.

A Diary of Unfinished Thoughts

My diary's filled with half-finished schemes,
Like puzzles that stare me down in my dreams.
I scribble and doodle, but clarity's shy,
Yet, who needs it? I'd rather fly high!

Each page a reminder of what's left undone,
But hey, ain't life better when it's all just fun?
So I'll raise a toast to messy old me,
Waving at chaos, my favorite spree!

Between the Now and Never

I'm stuck between a rock and a chair,
Wondering if I should comb my hair.
Life's a puzzle, pieces askew,
Do I laugh or just brew a brew?

Time ticks slowly, then it sprints,
The meaning's lost in subtle hints.
Should I dance or stick to the grind?
Shall I seek or just be blind?

Am I lost in thought or just plain lost?
Do I count my joys or weigh the cost?
A thought pops up, then it hops away,
Hello, goodbye—it's just my day!

So here I sit, sipping my tea,
Contemplating life's big mystery.
With each chuckle, I find my place,
In a bizarre, yet cozy space.

Chasing Fleeting Moments

Catch the bus that never arrives,
Wave goodbye to clever jives.
Moments fly like birds in spring,
I reach and grasp, but miss the wing.

The clock ticks loud, the tick-tock sings,
I search for meaning in little things.
A funny face, a little dance,
Erratic humor, fate's odd chance.

I wrote a list of things I want,
But all I got was a bad font.
Each item scribbled, lost in thought,
What I need is a well-timed shot!

So why not laugh at silly fate?
Smile wide as the hours wait.
Chase those moments, slyly run,
In life's circus, we're all the fun!

The Art of Unanswered Queries

Why is the sky blue? Why is it gray?
Questions pop up like a game we play.
I ask a lot, but know less yet,
Like trying to catch a cat in a net.

Can I cook spaghetti without a pot?
Does it matter? Not a whole lot!
Am I a genius or just pretend?
At questions' door, I always stand-end.

Should I ponder the stars or the crumbs?
When life feels like puns with no drums!
Every answer leads to more confusion,
Like socks that vanish—it's all an illusion!

So here's to queries, sharp and spry,
We laugh at truths that pass us by.
With humor bright, let's roll the dice,
In this riddle of life, I'll think twice!

Navigating the Sea of Meaning

In life's ocean, I'm a small boat,
Sailing through waves of silly thoughts.
With a map that's drawn in crayon hues,
I steer my course amidst the blues.

The sea of meaning ebbs and flows,
Tide pulls me fast, then leaves me froze.
Fish jump by, offering advice,
But their wisdom lacks that nice, warm spice!

What if I sail with eyes quite closed?
Would I be lost, or just well-posed?
Maybe dolphins whisper life's big score,
But all I hear? Just "try the shore!"

So here I float, not seeking fate,
Just tickling waves, it feels first-rate.
Navigating laughs on this wild spree,
In this ocean of jest, I'll just be me.

Seeking Solace in the Surreal

In dreams, I float on clouds of cheese,
Where time is just a game of tease.
A unicorn gives me stock advice,
But I can't afford my morning slice.

The moon wears socks, the stars all dance,
My cat's a philosopher; give him a chance.
He shrugs at life with a knowing glare,
As I sip soda from the midnight air.

The fridge hums secrets, keeps them tight,
A sandwich argues, "I'm your right!"
I chase my tail in this cosmic race,
And chuckle at the absurdity we face.

In this world, where logic takes a nap,
I find my joy in a colorful map.
Each crayon line leads me to silliness,
Where laughter erases the weight of this mess.

The Myth of Certainty

I woke up sure today was bright,
But the toaster disagreed outright.
It burned my toast like a fiery foe,
And now I'm stuck in the shadow of woe.

I wrote my goals in permanent ink,
But my pen ran dry; what do you think?
A fortune cookie told me to dive,
But it didn't say where I'd arrive.

Logic's a fool wearing a funny hat,
It scoffs at plans, like, "What's up with that?"
I try to grasp what's solid and real,
But even my shadow refuses to kneel.

In the land of doubt, I dance with glee,
Swapping certainties for sweet fantasy.
With every stumble and every fall,
I laugh like a child, who knows it all.

The Void in Our Coffee Cups

My morning brew whispers, "Life's a game,"
As I ponder caffeine like it's super fame.
I search for answers at the bottom of the cup,
But all I find is a soggy sad pup.

The sugar swirls like a dance-off spree,
While my mug grins, knowing more than me.
"Fill me up!" it chimes with a frothy cheer,
But the universe just rolls its sphere.

The cream floats like hope, then sinks like doubt,
In this latte labyrinth, what's it about?
I ask the barista if he knows the score,
He says, "Just drink it and maybe ask for more."

In every sip, a universe brews,
Of fleeting dreams and whimsical views.
And though I aim for a sip of the wise,
I'm left with foam and an empty surprise.

Questions Without Answers

Why do socks vanish in the laundry spin?
Did they enroll in a sock-topia win?
Is the sun a giant Hot Wheels track?
These queries linger, yet answers lack.

If life's a pie, are the slices sweet?
Are we all just crumbs in a dizzying feat?
What's the sound of one hand clapping its glee?
I raise my mug to the mystery!

Do fish dream of underwater fame?
Or do cats read books on nature's game?
The moon's a big lamp, but why so shy?
Are stars the universe's wink from the sky?

In the whirl of absurd, I giggle and sigh,
With every question, another cloud floats by.
Life's not a riddle I need to untie,
But a comedy show, with a well-timed lie.

Notes from the Edge of Beyond

Lost in thought and cosmic dust,
Why's the universe so robust?
Stars are winking, oh so sly,
Do they ponder? Oh me, oh my!

A couch of clouds, I take my seat,
With snack-shaped thoughts, oh what a treat!
Are we here for laughs or just for fun?
Or is it just a cosmic pun?

Sipping tea from a mug of fate,
Wondering why I just can't relate.
Are we all just bytes of code?
Clicking through this great abode?

Maybe I'm just a playful breeze,
Dancing in the cosmic freeze.
Laughing softly, what a ride,
On this wild and silly tide!

Breathing Through the Void

Floating softly through the air,
Is it my breath or just despair?
Counting moments, silly game,
Are we all just fans of fame?

Chasing shadows, what a sport,
In a universe that won't consort.
Who am I, a sock or shoe?
Do you wonder that, too?

Philosophers with fancy hats,
Pondering life and where it's at.
Each question's a riddle, you see,
Or just a joke—just let it be!

Breath of void, it gives a wink,
Filling pages with stinky ink.
Life's absurd, let's have some fun,
Until the cosmic joke is done!

The Gaps in Between

Filling gaps with bits of cheer,
Finding purpose far and near.
What exists in empty space?
Maybe just a funny face!

Questions bouncing like a ball,
Do they really matter at all?
In between the yes and no,
Maybe life's just one big show!

Chasing thoughts like feathered friends,
Which one to keep? Which one to send?
Life's a puzzle, I'm missing pieces,
But laughter's the glue that never ceases!

So here I stand on thought's great brink,
Curious creatures, what do you think?
Absurdity seems quite the trend,
Let's laugh together—life's a blend!

Sifting Through the Sands of Time

Sifting sands with shiny hands,
Hiding truths in shifting lands.
What's the meaning? Stop and stare,
Or are we just time's lost pair?

Tick-tock goes the cosmic clock,
Should I dance or just mock?
With each grain, a thought to weigh,
Or just a game we choose to play!

In a world of never-ending quests,
Finding joy in feeble jest.
Is the circus here to stay?
Or just a joke we laugh and play?

Sands of time are funny, dear,
Look closely, what might appear?
As moments drop, let's take a chance,
And join life's absurd dance!

Laughing at the Absurd

In a world so wacky, nothing makes sense,
A rubber chicken serves as my lens.
Why chase the goal when the road is the joke?
I'll dance with the chaos, life's whimsical poke.

The cat on the roof thinks it owns the street,
While I sip my coffee and ponder defeat.
With socks that don't match and a shoe that's too tight,
I'll embrace all the quirks that make living a plight.

When time starts to fly, I just wave it goodbye,
Like a bird on a wire, it's a whimsical lie.
Tick-tock goes the clock, but who's keeping score?
It's funny how little we're meant to explore.

So if life throws a curveball, just swing and you'll see,
The punchline is hidden, it's all just a spree.
With laughter in hand, I'll tip my tall hat,
Embracing the madness, and that's where it's at.

What Is It All For?

What is the meaning? Is there a prize?
A hamster on wheels, spinning 'til it cries.
Do we climb any ladders or stumble and fall?
Maybe it's just to have fun after all.

I read all the books, got dizzy with thoughts,
But nothing will clear up all the big knots.
I ask every mirror, 'What is the deal?'
The glass just reflects back my existential meal.

With coffee in hand and crumbs on my plate,
I ponder the cosmos while I contemplate.
Does the sun rise for me or just for a show?
I laugh at the question, 'What is it all for?'

So I'll dance with my doubts and twirl with my fears,
Singing nonsense to echo throughout the years.
If life is a riddle we can't really crack,
Let's turn up the music and never look back.

The Weight of a Single Thought

A single thought can weigh a ton,
Like an elephant trying to have fun.
The mind drags along, like molasses in air,
And I trip over dreams 'cause I'm lost in a stare.

Why fret over choices like shoes on the rack?
I'll wear one of each, there's no turning back.
With paradoxes danced from dusk until dawn,
I'll laugh at the weight and just carry on.

Do we ponder our purpose like sheep on the road?
While life plays the tune of a quirky old ode.
I'll juggle my worries, come join in my show,
Life's just a game, don't take it too slow.

So weigh your thoughts lightly, hold them with grace,
Like a feather that floats in a merry-go-race.
For in this mad circus, we're all in the fray,
Just juggle those thoughts, and let laughter play.

Unraveling the Fabric of Being

I tug at the thread of this life's crazy weave,
What's real? What's not? Is it all just a reprieve?
I'm knitting pot holders with questions galore,
Hoping the fabric has answers in store.

Let's unravel the yarn, see what's tangled inside,
Like spaghetti in sauce, let's take it in stride.
With each little loop, a new mystery grows,
Like socks in the dryer, who really knows?

As I tug on the truth, it slips through my hands,
Like ice cream on hot days, it just never stands.
I giggle at futures that never arrive,
It's the butterflies blushing that keep dreams alive.

So stitch up your laughter and wear it with pride,
We're weaving a tale where nonsense can glide.
Let's unravel forever, it's all in good fun,
For life is a quilt, and we're each a spun one.

Tales from the Abyss

In a void where socks go lost,
I ponder life's profound cost.
Are we but jokes in cosmic play?
Or just lost words in disarray?

I asked my cat, who stared and blinked,
She seemed to say, 'You've over-thinked!'
With cosmic questions in the air,
Do fish in water have the same despair?

Life's a ride on a crazy train,
With each stop, we feel some pain.
Yet laughter bursts like sunlight rays,
As we dance through this absurd maze.

So let's embrace the chaos here,
With silly hats and ice cream cheer.
In the abyss, we find our jest,
Being lost can be the best!

The Anatomy of Doubt

My brain's a carnival of fears,
Where doubts parade, to much loud cheers.
Do I exist, or just pretend?
Is life a book that has no end?

I read the signs; they say 'Be bold!'
Yet still I freeze like I'm quite cold.
Is it the coffee or my brain?
Both leave me wired and quite insane.

With every choice, a twist and turn,
A lesson taught, a page to burn.
Should I leap or just sit tight?
Oh, the fun in losing sight!

So here's to doubts, we raise a glass,
To all the questions that we amass.
Let's laugh at life's grand carousel,
For in confusion, we find our spell!

A Canvas of Choices

Each morning greets with shades of fate,
A palette mixed in a cosmic state.
Should I wear blue or daring red?
Choices linger in my head.

I could be rich or maybe poor,
Stay inside or roam the shore.
Life's a painting, a wild stroke,
Where logic laughs and senses choke.

Choose vanilla or chocolate scoop,
In this absurd and silly loop.
What's the plan? Who even knows?
Let's just dance and strike a pose!

So let's paint life with vibrant hues,
Embrace the chaos, pick your muse.
In every choice, a chance to smile,
Silly canvases are worth the while!

Conversations with the Infinite

Late at night, I ponder deep,
Does the cosmos ever sleep?
I asked the stars, they winked and shone,
'Just chill, my friend, you're not alone.'

I chat with moons and comets bright,
While sipping tea by candlelight.
Do they giggle at our trivia?
Or do they think we're all just via?

'What's the secret?' I start to plead,
The void just laughs, it has no speed.
They say the answer's in your heart,
Yet I still feel like I'm not smart.

So I'll keep talking, night through day,
To all the stars, I'll have my say.
In every chuckle, wisdom's caught,
Life's a comedy — we're all just bought!

A Journey Through the Uncertain

In a world where questions sprout,
We wander round with brains in doubt.
With every step, a choice to make,
But is the path a piece of cake?

What if penguins wore a tie?
And talked philosophy on the fly?
They'd surely have a lot to say,
About why we're lost—hip hip hooray!

Should I take the road less traveled?
Or just stay home and watch it unraveled?
Each signpost leads to a new twist,
Yet I'd prefer to eat and resist!

But in this maze, let's have some fun,
With every riddle that weighs a ton.
So let's laugh hard and let thoughts spout,
As we journey through the certainties—about!

The Poetry of Absence

My sock's gone missing, oh what a plight,
It vanished without a hint or a bite.
Perhaps it learned the dance of the void,
While I sit here feeling quite annoyed.

Absence, like a ghost, gives a sly wink,
It teases my mind, makes me rethink.
Do I ponder deep or just take a snack?
In emptiness, I plan the next attack.

Oh, where's my motivation? I've lost the thread!
A phantom of focus dances instead.
With each empty thought, I slowly sway,
In the poetry of absence, I'll nap all day!

The fridge hums a tune, a comforting sound,
It sings of leftovers waiting to be found.
So here's to absence, that sneaky ol' friend,
At least I've got snacks, let the thinking suspend!

Reflections in a Broken Mirror

Oh dear reflection, what do you see?
A jumbled mess, is that really me?
Shattered pieces, some might object,
But hey, looks are just a tiny aspect.

The mirror cracked while I posed just right,
And suddenly my hair's a fright!
Is this the self that I once adored?
Or just a version I can't afford?

Love handles and angles, all askew,
Why don't you try a different view?
In every shard, a truth lies near,
That laughter's better than the fear!

With winks and pouts, I take a stand,
In this funny game, it's just quite grand.
So let's embrace every quirky flaw,
In a broken mirror, we'll find our awe!

Navigating the Labyrinth of Self

Lost in a maze that's all my own,
With paths and corners I've never known.
A sign that says, 'Go left, not right!'
But what if left is just a fright?

My thoughts like breadcrumbs drop and roll,
In this twisted mind, I'm on patrol.
Oh look, there's doubt, with a map and pen,
Anxiety laughs, 'Let's do it again!'

I asked a minotaur for some advice,
He said, 'Just dance, it's rather nice.'
So I twirled round in confusion and grace,
In this labyrinth of self, I found my place.

Let's make a game of all this stress,
Where every wrong turn is mere finesse.
With humor as my trusty guide,
Navigating shall be my joy and pride!

Dancing on the Edge of Reason

In a world where thoughts collide,
I twirl on logic's shaded side.
With a wink and a little jig,
I laugh at life, it's all so big.

The clock ticks loud, a mocking tune,
Yet I dance 'neath a silver moon.
With each misstep, wisdom falls,
And I just grin—who really calls?

Rationality's a tightrope thin,
Balancing dreams and goofy grins.
So let them judge, their faces stoned,
I'm the jester on the throne!

Embrace the chaos, sway and play,
Reason's rules can fade away.
A chuckle here, a snort or two,
In this waltz, I'll never rue!

Emptiness and Echoes

In a void where silence sings,
I trip over my own musings.
Echoes bounce off empty walls,
Who knew thoughts could drop like balls?

A hollow laugh, a silent cheer,
What's that noise? Oh, it's just fear.
Yet here I sit, a cup of tea,
Wondering if 'me' is just 'me.'

Philosophers whisper and scheme,
While I'm caught in a half-baked dream.
I ask the void, "What's up with you?"
It giggles back, "Just passing through!"

So raise a glass to emptiness bright,
And let's toast to absurd delight!
For in the echoes, laughter finds,
A punchline lost between our minds.

The Search for Meaning in a Crowded Room

In a room full of chatter and cheer,
I search for meaning, drink a beer.
Conversations whirl like a dance,
Yet no one seems to take a chance.

"Hey, what's life?" I ask a grandma,
She smiles wide, "More drama than a saga!"
I nod sagely, but still confused,
In a sea of fades, I feel used.

A fellow laughs, "Is this a joke?"
"No, my friend, just a life cloak!"
He shrugs it off, returns to snack,
And I sit here, still looking back.

In the crowd, those who seek escape
Find solace in their own landscape.
So let's all laugh and share the gloom,
Together searching in this room!

Shadows of Certainty

What's certain in this quirky place?
Shadows dance with a goofy grace.
I chase the dark with sheer delight,
As reason slips into the night.

With logic tied in knots so tight,
I stumble on, questioning light.
Certainties laugh, a playful tease,
While I just shrug, "Oh, life's a breeze!"

A shadow whispers, "You're all aglow!"
I nod, unsure, "But where's the show?"
In every doubt, a hint of fun,
While dancing shadows weave and run.

So let's embrace the silly and wild,
Where certainties get utterly mild.
In laughter's grip, we'll find our way,
Through shadows bright, come what may!

The Elusiveness of Certainty

In a world that spins and sways,
We chase the truth in many ways.
Just when you think you've got it right,
A curveball whizzes into sight.

The answers hide like socks in the wash,
You're certain, then—whoosh!—it's a nosh.
With every step, we second-guess,
A simple truth turns into a mess.

Knowing nothing's which we can thrive,
In doubt, we feel very much alive.
So here's a wink to all those who search,
The truth's a prank that plays in the lurch.

So let's toast to this carnival ride,
Where certainty's just a happy slide.
We'll tumble down and giggle absurd,
For answers are passé and honestly blurred.

Finding Meaning in the Mundane

In coffee spills and traffic jams,
We seek the gold in daily whams.
A sock's lost, and it starts a quest,
To find a reason—who needs the rest?

Dust bunnies dance, what a nice surprise,
They hold secret worlds behind our eyes.
The cat on the couch is a zen-like sage,
With wisdom tucked neatly on each page.

Each little moment, a potential giggle,
Like finding a tune in the hardest wiggle.
So we toast to the ordinary glee,
For meaning's not grand; it's just having tea.

So laugh at the chaos, adore the grind,
In the silly ordinary, joy is easy to find.
Life's a wild sketch with doodles and swirls,
We're just comic strips in this world of twirls.

The Inevitability of Contradiction

In a land where yes always means no,
We juggle our thoughts in a baffling show.
You can't have your cake and eat it too,
But that's just an invitation to chew!

Words twist and turn like a playful cat,
'Till logic unravels, and we're all flat.
Truth takes a nap, leaves doubt in the air,
We stumble around without a care.

The scholar and jester share a fine drink,
In this merry world that makes you think.
So raise a glass to our goofy plight,
Where contradictions dance through the night.

Laughter bubbles up when we embrace the mess,
For life's quirky chaos, we must confess.
The more we fumble, the more we ignite,
A circus of thought, a whimsical fight.

Dilemmas of the Unspeakable

We sit and ponder what we can't say,
Like guessing secrets meant for the play.
Awkward pauses in a hilarious chat,
Are we human or just a big spat?

With frowns and giggles, we spin our tales,
In the land of 'what ifs' and 'forgotten mails.'
What lurks beneath all those social masks?
Just a bunch of clowns avoiding tough tasks.

We tackle truths like juggling knives,
Balancing thoughts, but oh, how it thrives!
In silence, the awkwardness finds a spark,
A raucous laugh, brightening the dark.

So raise your hand if you dare to speak,
Join in the mayhem of the mild and the meek.
In dilemmas' depths, we find the fun,
A dance with the unspeakable, we've just begun!

A Traveler's Guide to Nowhere

Pack your bags, but stay right here,
All roads lead to where? Oh dear!
Maps all crumpled, directions lost,
Finding meaning comes at a cost.

Get your passport stamped for a laugh,
The universe is one big gaffe.
With every turn, the questions rise,
Answers hide behind cloudy skies.

The destination's a riddle to solve,
In circles we dance, problems evolve.
Just pack your whimsy and you'll see,
Nowhere's the place to truly be free.

So raise a toast to the paths we tread,
Seeking wisdom in what's unsaid.
For life's a trip, we all can share,
Even if we get stuck in air.

Flickers of Reality

Reality's a flickering light,
On, off, like a switch in the night.
What's real, what's fake? Take your pick,
It's all a game, and life's the trick.

You're a ghost in a human shell,
Complaining, laughing, ringing the bell.
Asking questions with no clear aim,
Each answer dampens the flaming game.

Reality's just a punchline now,
With logic seated, taking a bow.
The absurd is where we take our stand,
Juggling meanings like grains of sand.

So dance with shadows and take a leap,
For truth is a jest, and it's yours to keep.
Flickers of brightness — don't miss the show,
In this wacky world, just go with the flow.

The Weight of Being

Feeling heavy? It's all in your mind,
The weight of being's unkind.
With every thought, the load will grow,
But laughter lightens what we know.

We carry dreams like rocks in a bag,
Tripping over thoughts that nag.
It's hard to breathe, so take a shot,
At finding joys in what you've got.

Life's a stage, and we all play parts,
Hiding smiles behind hearty farts.
So lighten up, dear wandering soul,
You're more than the weight; just take a stroll.

The burdens shift; they come and go,
Like socks that vanish in the laundry flow.
So cheer up, friend, shake off that gloom,
For being is better with a laugh and a room.

In the Company of Forgotten Thoughts

Lost ideas that wander astray,
Join a club that's full of dismay.
Forgotten thoughts are buzzing bees,
Swarming around with labored ease.

They scratch their heads and mumble loud,
While we just nod, so very proud.
Chasing wisps like summer's breeze,
Inane insights, with minds like cheese.

In the company of what's left behind,
We laugh and cringe at our own mind.
Those silly tales, once so profound,
Transform to giggles; they know no bound.

So gather round, let's share a chuckle,
With nostalgia's sting, let it buckle.
For lost thoughts are still our favorite guests,
They bring the fun and all the best.

The Ponderer's Dilemma

Why's the sky so blue, I muse?
What's the deal with human views?
Bake a cake or write a book?
Such a quandary, what a hook!

Coffee brews beneath the sun,
While I ponder, where's the fun?
Should I dance or take a nap?
Oh dear, life's quite the trap!

Each small choice, a mountain made,
Will I fail or get parayed?
A sock drawer full of despair,
Or the cosmos in my hair?

But I'll laugh as I explore,
This wild maze that I adore.
Grab a snack, forget the fuss,
Life's a ride, just hop on bus!

In Search of the Lost Why

Why do we eat, sleep, and play?
Is there meaning? Who can say?
Maybe it's all a big joke,
Like a clown in a white smoke!

Maps are drawn, my compass spins,
Chasing answers where it begins.
With every step, a question blooms,
Like a plant that could fill rooms!

What's the point of 9 to 5?
Is it just to feel alive?
Or is it just a cosmic prank,
Like a fish that swims in ink?

So I laugh at these lost whys,
While searching for truth under lies.
Sip my tea, take a puff,
Life's a riddle, is it tough?

Acomplices of Absurdity

Caught in chaos, hold my hand,
We'll explore this silly land.
Life's a farce, or so they say,
So let's dance the day away!

Why wear shoes if feet are fine?
The world's a stage, we're all on line.
With each mishap and every fall,
We giggle loud, we stand tall!

Grab your hats and join the fun,
Let's make mischief, just for one!
Wit and whimsy our daily bread,
As we tumble 'round our head!

In this absurd, chaotic spree,
We find joy in irony.
Raise a toast to life's weird game,
We're the fools, but it's the same!

The Path Less Understood

Stumble down the winding road,
What's that light? A flashing code!
With every twist, a joke unfolds,
Like old socks or tales retold.

Where's the path that makes more sense?
Like math with a little suspense.
Do I travel north or south,
Or just follow my silly mouth?

I could stay, but where's the thrill?
Or take the chance, embrace the chill?
Life's a puzzle, pieces stray,
Let's put 'em back in a funny way!

So here's to paths, both clear and strange,
With every step, let's rearrange.
Laugh aloud through thick and thin,
Dancing down the path we spin!

Chronicles of the Indifferent Universe

In a vast cosmic joke, we float and we spin,
Stars twinkle, yet they just don't care,
Gravity's cling is a clumsy lover,
While we mix cocktails of chaos and air.

Planets gossip and comets collide,
Yet here we are, debating our fate,
A speck on a rock, we dance and we sigh,
In this grand theater where none hold a plate.

The sun rises up, like it's on a clock,
While clouds are indifferent, just passing by,
Life's a sitcom, no pause or replay,
Strap in, everyone, it's a wild ride!

So here's to the void that feels like home,
We fit right in with our capable fumbles,
With each sip of absurdity we're free,
In this indifferent universe, we happily grumble.

Reflections of a Curious Heart

I woke up this morning with questions anew,
Why do we tick like poorly made clocks?
Is life a puzzle, or perhaps a riddle?
More like a sock drawer, cluttered with shocks.

Oh, to be curious, what a delightful spree,
Questions like sprinkles on ice cream delight,
I asked a goldfish, but it swam away,
Fish don't engage, they're a bit too polite!

Can aliens see us, with their scopes and their beams?
Do they laugh at our awkward dance moves all night?
We ponder existence while sipping our brews,
As the universe giggles—oh, what a sight!

So let's toast to the questions that tickle our brains,
In the land of the curious where wonders abound,
Keep asking and laughing, it's all part of the game,
In this big comedy show, we're joyfully drowned.

When Thoughts Wander

Thoughts wander off like a lost puppy's chase,
They fetch confusion, then roll in the mud,
Searching for answers in places they shouldn't,
Like socks in the dryer, all tangled and flood.

My brain's a circus, with clowns on a ride,
Explanations tumble like acrobats bold,
I ponder the meaning, the why and the how,
While popcorn explodes, the day turns to gold.

Do they have a map, these thoughts on the run?
Or just a vague feeling of where they might go?
Chasing their tails, they blend in the fun,
A lively parade, though it may be low brow!

Yet in this messy, chaotic escapade,
There's beauty in riddle, absurdity reigns,
So when thoughts wander, let them roam wide,
It's a party for one, and we're dancing in chains!

Living in the Shadows of Our Minds

In the attic of thoughts, cobwebs reside,
Whispers of worries and dreams stack on high,
Here, shadows dance a quirky ballet,
While our minds play peekaboo, soaring and shy.

We juggle our fears like a circus of doubt,
With every big thought, a tiny one slips,
Worry's a waiter at our mind's dinner party,
Pouring us cocktails of panic with sips.

We're all just actors in this twisty play,
Pretending we know all our lines and our marks,
But laughter's the key to unlock this charade,
So let's throw confetti and dance with the sparks!

So here's to the shadows, let them be wild,
Finding joy in chaos—a child's delight,
In the labyrinth of our quirky old minds,
Let's frolic through thoughts, from day into night.

Portraits of the Unknowable

In a gallery of quirks and gaffes,
Hang the faces of the baffled laughs.
Each canvas a puzzle, a riddle in time,
Smiling at questions that seem so sublime.

A wobbly frame beneath a big hat,
A stick figure pondering where they are at.
With colors that clash and brushes that sway,
They wonder aloud if it's all just play.

Art that giggles and shrugs with delight,
Why existential crises give us a fright?
"Who am I?" they ask, with a wink and a grin,
While the answer throws confetti, let the games begin!

So hang up your toys alongside the deep,
In the art of confusion, there's nothing to keep.
With each stroke of humor, we dance through the grey,
In the portraits of ponderers—let's frolic away!

The Path of the Questioner

On a winding road of queries galore,
The path zigzags, inviting us to explore.
With a backpack of doubts and a map full of why,
Let's walk and let laughter be our alibi.

Down the trail of 'What if?' we skip with mirth,
As our heads spin around like they're on a dearth.
"Is it all just a game?" we giggle and cheer,
Where answers play peek-a-boo, somehow unclear.

Each step is a riddle, a raucous good laugh,
As we stumble through riddles on a quirky path.
"Can trees really talk?" we yell with a tease,
The trees shrug back, "Dude, do as you please."

A parade of questions marching in style,
With absurdities leading us mile after mile.
So grab your buddy and walk hand in hand,
On the path of the curious, let joy be the plan!

Whispers of an Unsung Fate

In a café of dreams where the shadows convene,
Coffee cups whisper secrets, both silly and keen.
"What lies ahead?" they ponder, in sips and in slurps,
As fortune cookies giggle, their humor in burps.

The barista smirks, pouring fate with a flair,
"Extra foam for the brave who dare to care!"
With everyoo, a chuckle, a twist of the spoon,
In the theater of chaos, we dance to the tune.

A clock hangs askew, its hands all askance,
Time bursts into laughter while giving a chance.
"What's next?" we inquire with a wink and a grin,
The answer's a shrug — might as well begin!

So raise up your glass to the unknown galore,
In whispers of fate, there's always room for more.
With humor our compass, we toast to the night,
In the chaos of living, let's soar to the light!

Moments Suspended in Time

In a bubble of laughter, time takes a pause,
Suspended in giggles, it catches applause.
Each second a joke, dangling out like a string,
What fun as we dangle, let joy be the king!

A moment of chaos, where cats write a song,
And cacti in tutus help us get along.
We freeze in a snapshot of curious delight,
As the world spins around us, we bask in the light.

Imagine a clock with hands made of jelly,
Tickling the moments that bounce like a belly.
Time wears a smile, no flaws in the rhyme,
In the playground of seconds, let's savor the climb.

So wrap up your worries, let laughter dictate,
These moments are treasures, they're perfectly great.
In the fabric of time, we're woven with glee,
Suspended forever, just you wait and see!

Discovering Life in the Inconsequential

A crumb on the floor, oh the joy it could bring,
It's a feast for the ants, let the party begin!
We fret and we worry about grand, lofty things,
While nature's small wonders make our hearts sing.

Why chase after clouds when a pebble can shine?
The meaning of life's in a dandelion's line.
We ponder the cosmos, it's vast and it's grand,
But I found more wisdom in a child's outstretched hand.

When the Stars Don't Speak

I looked at the stars, asked them what's it all for,
They twinkled and said, "We're just glowing galore!"
No answers in light, just a stardust parade,
Maybe they're waiting for a cosmic charade.

A black hole's a mystery, a void without sound,
While I can't even find my lost keys in this town.
The heavens know nothing of my midnight plight,
I'll blame them for silence—oh, that feels just right!

The Art of Questioning Everything

Why is the moon yellow? And why is grass green?
Do cats have a secret that we've never seen?
I ponder the meaning of socks in the dryer,
Is a life without questions just one big flat tire?

Why is the coffee always strong and so bleak?
Does the universe giggle when we're feeling weak?
I'll ask all the wonders while I sip on my brew,
For the joy is in questioning, at least that much is true!

What Lies Beyond the Horizon?

Is it more of the same, or a land made of cheese?
Do unicorns dance there, floating soft on the breeze?
With binoculars firm, I squint at the view,
The horizon is winking, what's a dreamer to do?

Perhaps it's a place where socks always match,
And Mondays are friendly, with a warm, cozy hatch.
Or maybe it's just more of the daily grind,
Yet my heart races faster; it's hope that I find!

A Guide to Life's Nothingness

The universe is vast and wide,
We question where we fit inside.
A speck of dust, we float and sway,
But hey, at least it's a fun display!

The coffee brews, the toast will burn,
We ponder life and take a turn.
Is there a point to all this fuss?
Or just a cosmic game for us?

We laugh at days that come and go,
While searching for a secret glow.
A treasure map with no clear prize,
But humor makes us wise and spry!

So here's to life, a whirling ride,
With questions bouncing far and wide.
We'll dance along the edge of woe,
And giggle at the great unknown!

The Art of Unknowing

We wake each day, the same old grind,
With thoughts that drift and twist our mind.
What's the secret? What's the catch?
Oh look, a squirrel! Let's watch it snatch!

In life's grand book, we miss a page,
Embrace the chaos, unleash the rage.
Perhaps the truth's a cruel prank,
So let's just laugh, it's all we bank!

The experts talk, but who can tell?
We wander through this quirky shell.
A guide to nothing? Who needs that?
I'll take a nap, or chase my cat!

With all these ponderings, so profound,
We often find we're lost, not found.
Yet in this maze, we find delight,
The art of unknowing feels just right!

Soliloquy of the Soul

Oh soul of mine, so filled with dread,
Is there a meaning? Or just bread?
I ponder deeply, spill my thoughts,
But what I find is all for naught.

In shadows cast by thoughts so bleak,
I hunt for answers, yet feel weak.
A whisper says, 'Just take a seat,'
And see the world beneath your feet.

A dance of bliss, a silly spin,
The meaning slips, then slips again.
So here I stand, quite lost, but bold,
Embracing all the strange and cold.

With every sigh, a chuckle brews,
In this absurdity, I choose.
My soul's soliloquy may roam,
But in this chaos, I feel at home!

Defining Purpose in a Sea of Randomness

In seas of random, we set afloat,
Searching for meaning in this big boat.
A fish could swim, but why's it there?
Perhaps to flaunt its aquatic flair!

We ponder stars and cones of ice,
Each question asked, the same old spice.
What's my purpose? I ask aloud,
The universe shrugs; it's feeling proud.

In moments sweet, in moments strange,
We laugh at life, embrace the change.
So slip and slide into the mess,
And dance while wearing your old dress!

For in this randomness, we sway,
Making meaning in a funny way.
Defining life in chuckles and fun,
In this great play, we're all but one!

Beyond the Veil of Understanding

In a coffee shop, I sip and stare,
Wondering if I'm really there.
Is that my latte, or just the dream?
Oh look, there's my soulmate on a screen!

Questions tumble like sugar cubes,
Falling through cracks, making new moods.
The universe laughs, what a great jest!
I'm just a puzzle, trying my best.

What's the meaning of life, they say?
Is it found in sushi or a cabaret?
Maybe it's hidden in a dad's joke,
Or in that ridiculous hat I broke.

So I sit and ponder, sip my brew,
Reading the labels on my shoe.
The mysteries swirl like cream in my cup,
And I toast the absurdity—cheers, what's up?

The Space Between Thoughts

Thoughts are like birds, they fly and chirp,
But sometimes they trip, and that's quite the burp!
I catch myself thinking of pizza and fries,
Why do we ponder? Don't ask, just try!

In the quiet moments, it all feels so vast,
Like a sock lost in laundry—never to cast.
I wrestle with answers that dance in a line,
While my brain nods off, saying, 'Hey, I'm fine!'

Ideas pop up like popcorn in air,
Some are plain goofy, without a care.
The void means nothing—oh what a treat!
Except for the bill we forget to meet.

Between the thoughts, there's laughter and glee,
Mixed with deep musings and some spilled tea.
So raise your glass to this weird little ride,
And embrace the weirdness that lives inside!

Searching for Signs in the Void

I stare at the stars, looking for clues,
Are they directions or just cosmic snooze?
The moon gives a wink, as if to say,
'Chill out, my friend, just enjoy the play!'

I chalk up my worries to weather's decree,
Is today sunny, or just wrong for me?
The wind blows nonsense that tickles my ear,
As I question my purpose with half a cold beer.

Post-it notes scatter, a roadmap of sorts,
One says 'Donuts', another 'Don't short'.
I laugh and I pet my philosophical cat,
Are we really that deep, or just chasing a hat?

So, I search for the signs, like a kid in a park,
And wonder if wisdom is just a lark.
Between clueless giggles and queries so bold,
The void whispers softly, 'Hey, behold!'

Embracing the Paradox

I'm told I'm lost, but where is my map?
Could it be hiding in some cosmic gap?
I juggle my thoughts like a clown at a fair,
Balancing sanity with a pinch of despair.

Life's a riddle, or maybe a prank,
Like stepping in gum on the way to the bank.
The truth's a mischief-maker, causing commotion,
A fish riding bikes in a vast ocean.

I can't help but chuckle at this grand charade,
Where doubts are confetti, all brightly displayed.
Every answer becomes a new twisty trail,
Full of laughter echoes, like wind in a sail.

So let's dance in the chaos, embrace the absurd,
With wink and a nod, let's sing every word.
The paradox beckons, come take a swing,
As life's just a giggle in a cosmic fling!

Echoes of the Unasked

Why are we here, in this chair?
Staring at the ceiling, with a blank stare.
Is it deep thought or just plain dread?
Or did I forget what my dog just said?

Questions float like balloons in the sky,
Tangled and twisting as the birds fly by.
If a tree falls and no one can hear,
Does it write a memoir on existential fear?

In search of meaning, we trip on our shoelaces,
Trading our thoughts for awkward embraces.
Like kids in a playground, with swings that creak,
We ponder our purpose, but can't even speak.

So here's to the baffled, the lost, the confused,
With snacks in our pockets, we're simply amused.
Let's laugh at the chaos, it's part of the game,
In this playground of thought, we're all feeling the same.

Calibrating Our Collective Confusion

Let's recalibrate our wobbly plots,
Measure the value of all our thoughts.
On this cosmic scale, we're all a bit lost,
Trading our sanity for digital costs.

Life feels like a sitcom with no clear script,
Our punchlines fail as sanity slips.
With popcorn in hand, we watch and we grin,
Wondering how silly we were to begin.

Riding the waves of uncertainty's tide,
Reaching for meaning, it's quite the ride.
We gather our questions like socks on the floor,
Each one is a mystery we can't ignore.

So raise your glass, here's to our plight,
In this grand circus, we dance in the night.
Let's celebrate nonsense, it's part of the fun,
In this collective chaos, we're all just one.

Fables of Fleeting Existence

Gather 'round, let's spin a tale,
Of wobbly existence, like a boat without a sail.
A fish once dreamed of being a bird,
But flapped its fins and got quite absurd.

In a world where time is but a jest,
We chase after moments, never at rest.
Like donuts disappearing in a morning haze,
Our laughter's the light that guides our ways.

Once, a wise turtle asked a sly fox,
"Why are your thoughts like ticking clocks?"
Fox shrugged and laughed, "I just enjoy the chase,
In a race against time, I'll win with grace!"

So here's to fables of things we can't see,
With each twist and turn, come roll along with me.
For in this mad world, we scribble our tunes,
And float through existence like dandelion moons.

The Stillness of the Infinite

In the stillness, where thoughts do collide,
We ponder the vastness, yet we can't decide.
Is the universe laughing, or just lost in a nap?
Or are we the punchline of some cosmic crap?

Stars twinkle brightly, like winking eyes,
Are they sharing secrets, or just telling lies?
Our whispers echo in the void so deep,
While we search for answers, a promise to keep.

In moments of silence, we dance with the weight,
Juggling our doubts, while debating our fate.
Like clumsy ninjas under the moon's silver light,
We laugh at the absurdity of our plight.

So sit back and revel in the quiet of night,
Where stillness and chaos both take flight.
In the infinite jest, we're all just a part,
Finding humor and joy in the questions of art.

www.ingramcontent.com/pod-product-compliance
Lightning Source LLC
Chambersburg PA
CBHW071847160426
43209CB00003B/456